Nelson Comprehension
Pupil Book 1

Wendy Wren
Series Editor: John Jackman

OXFORD
UNIVERSITY PRESS

Great Clarendon Street, Oxford, OX2 6DP, United Kingdom

Oxford University Press is a department of the University of Oxford.
It furthers the University's objective of excellence in research, scholarship,
and education by publishing worldwide. Oxford is a registered trade mark of
Oxford University Press in the UK and in certain other countries

Text © Wendy Wren 2009
Original illustrations © Oxford University Press 2014

The moral rights of the authors have been asserted

First published by Nelson Thornes Ltd in 2009
This edition published by Oxford University Press in 2014

All rights reserved. No part of this publication may be reproduced,
stored in a retrieval system, or transmitted, in any form or by any
means, without the prior permission in writing of Oxford University
Press, or as expressly permitted by law, by licence or under terms
agreed with the appropriate reprographics rights organization.
Enquiries concerning reproduction outside the scope of the above
should be sent to the Rights Department, Oxford University Press, at
the address above.

You must not circulate this work in any other form and you must
impose this same condition on any acquirer

British Library Cataloguing in Publication Data
Data available

978-1-4085-0546-5

7

Printed in China

Acknowledgements

Illustrations: Gustavo Mazali, Mike Phillips, Pedro Penizzotto, Iole Rosa, Simon Rumble, François Ruyer, Martin Sanders (all c/o Beehive Illustration), Mike Bastin, Mark Draisey, Paul McCaffrey (c/o Sylvie Poggio Artists Agency), Andy Peters Illustrators, and Wrexham County Borough Council
Photos: Fotolia, p53; Chloë Gathern, p25; all other photos, Istockphoto.com
Cover image: François Ruyer (c/o Beehive Illustration)
Page layout: Topics – The Creative Partnership, Exeter

The author and publisher are grateful to the following for permission to reproduce copyright material:

[Unit 1 Teach] extract from A. Forsyth, *The Laughing Snowman*, first published in the UK by Hodder Children's Books, a division of Hachette Children's Books, 338 Euston Road, London, NW1 3BH; [Unit 1 Talk] extract from M. Mahy, *The Door in the Air and Other Stories*, Watson Little Ltd. (agents); [Unit 1 Write] extract from P. Lively, *Uninvited Ghosts*, Heinemann; [Unit 3 Teach] *The Shape I'm in* © 2002 James Carter, from CARS STARS ELECTRIC GUITARS by James Carter, Reproduced by permission of Walker Books Ltd, London SE11 5HJ; [Unit 3 Teach] *Cats Can* taken from *C. Rumble, The Works*, first published by Macmillan; [Unit 3 Talk] *Rhythm Machine* © Trevor Harvey, first published in *Techno-talk: Poems with Byte*, 1994, Bodley Head; [Unit 3 Write] *Stereo Headphones* © 2002 James Carter, from CARS STARS ELECTRIC GUITARS by James Carter, Reproduced by permission of Walker Books Ltd, London SE11 5HJ; [Unit 7 Teach] extract from *Rent a Friend* by Frieda Hughes, first published in the UK by Hodder Children's Books, a division of Hachette Children's Books, 338 Euston Road, London, NW1 3BH; [Unit 7 Write] extract from Phyllis Arkle, *The Village Dinosaur*, reproduced with permission of Hodder and Stoughton Limited; [Unit 9 Write] images and text extract from *Recycle with Michael*, used with kind permission of Wrexham County Borough Council; [Unit 10] extracts from *Dragon Ride* by Helen Cresswell (© Helen Cresswell, 1989), reprinted by permission of A M Heath and Co. Ltd. Authors' Agents.

Although we have made every effort to trace and contact all
copyright holders before publication this has not been possible in all
cases. If notified, the publisher will rectify any errors or omissions at
the earliest opportunity.

Links to third party websites are provided by Oxford in good faith
and for information only. Oxford disclaims any responsibility for
the materials contained in any third party website referenced in
this work.

Contents

Unit 1 **Familiar places** 4

Unit 2 **Finding the facts** 10

Unit 3 **Odd-looking poems!** 16

Unit 4 **Let's find out!** 22

Unit 5 **Perseus's quest** 28

Unit 6 **How can we do that?** 34

Unit 7 **Talk, talk, talk!** 40

Unit 8 **You have to read this!** 46

Unit 9 **Can I change your mind?** 52

Unit 10 **What's going to happen next?** 58

How to use this book **64**

Unit 1

Familiar places
- Understanding settings in stories
- Drawing on prior knowledge

The Laughing Snowman

It is going to snow but Emma is the only one in her family who is excited about this. What do you think she will do in the snow?

'We'll have snow **before long**,' said Dad, looking up at the sky.

'Snow,' said Mum and she shivered.

'Snow,' said Emma's sister Mandy. 'Well, I won't go out. I'll stay indoors by the fire.'

'Snow!' said Emma. 'We haven't had snow for years!'

All day at school, she kept looking out of the window, watching for the first snowflakes. It got colder and colder, but still it didn't snow.

That night, when she was snuggled down under the duvet, Emma meant to stay awake – just in case it snowed during the night. But in ten minutes she was **fast asleep.**

When she woke up the next morning, she knew right away that something had happened. There was a strange silence. Usually she could hear the rumble of the traffic **in the distance**. Often there was the sound of a car engine spluttering into life across the way. But this morning it was very quiet.

Emma jumped out of bed and flung open the curtains.

All over the garden was a soft downy covering of pure white. Snow hung like icing sugar along the branches of the tree by the gate.

She ran through to wake up Mum and Dad. 'It's snowed! Get up! Look!'

'Mmm …' said Dad.

'Uh-huh,' said Mum. They didn't seem a bit interested. So she went to tell Mandy.

'Go away!' Mandy mumbled sleepily. 'It's Saturday.'

The Laughing Snowman,
Anne Forsyth

> - What was Mandy going to do if it snowed?
> - Why did Emma want to stay awake that night?
> - What was strange when Emma woke up the next morning?
> - What day did it snow?
> - Where was Emma when she said, 'We haven't had snow for years!'
> - What do the phrases in bold mean?
> - How do you know that Emma was the only one excited about the snow?
> - Look at the title of the story. What do you think Emma did that day?
> - How do you feel about snow? What do you do when it snows?

Unit 1

The House of Coloured Windows

This story describes ordinary houses on an ordinary street … except for one extraordinary house.

Our street had a lot of little houses on either side of it where we children lived happily with our families. There were rows of lawns, like green napkins tucked under the houses' chins, and letterboxes, apple trees and marigolds. Children played up and down the street, laughing and shouting and sometimes crying, for it's the way of the world that things should be mixed. In the soft autumn evenings before winter winds began, the smoke from the chimneys rose up in threads of grey and blue, stitching our houses into the autumn air.

 Understanding the passage
- Name four things that the houses had.
- Where did the children play?
- Were the children always happy? How do you know?
- Which house was different from the other houses?
- How was it different?

Looking at words
Explain the meaning of the words as they are used in the story:
  napkins   threads   wizard

But there was one house in our street that was different from all the rest, and that was the wizard's house. For one thing there was a door knocker of iron in the shape of a dog's head that barked at us as we ran by. Of course, the wizard's house had its lawn too, but no apple trees or marigolds, only a silver tree with a golden parrot in it. But that was not the most wonderful thing about the wizard's house.

The House of Coloured Windows,
Margaret Mahy

Looking at story settings
- What setting is being described?
- What happens in the autumn?
- What is the weather like in winter?
- The lawns are described as 'green napkins tucked under the houses' chins'. Is this a good description? Why? Why not?
- Explain why you would or would not like to live in a street like this.
- Look at the title of the story. What do you think might be 'the most wonderful thing' about the wizard's house?

 Extra

Describe where you live. What do you like about it?
What don't you like about it?

Uninvited Ghosts

This story describes the day the Brown family move house, and something very strange happens.
Marion and Simon were sent to bed early on the day that the Brown family moved house. By then everyone had lost their temper with everyone else; the cat had been sick on the sitting-room carpet; the dog had run away twice. If you have ever moved house you will know what kind of day it had been. Packing cases and newspaper all over the place … sandwiches instead of proper meals … the kettle lost and a wardrobe stuck on the stairs and Mrs Brown's favourite vase broken. There was bread and baked beans for supper, the television wouldn't work and the water wasn't hot so when all was said and done the children didn't object too violently to being packed off to bed. They'd had enough, too. They had one last argument about who was going to sleep by the window, put on their pyjamas, got into bed, switched the lights off … and it was at that point the ghost came out of the bottom drawer of the chest of drawers.

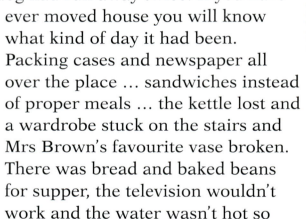

Uninvited Ghosts, **Penelope Lively**

Understanding the passage
  1 a What had the Brown family done that day?
    b What had the cat done?
  2 What happened to Mrs Brown's favourite vase?
  3 What did they have for supper?
  4 What strange thing happened when the children went to bed?

Looking at words
  5 Explain the meaning of these words and phrases as they are used in the story:
    a lost their temper   b packing cases   c all over the place
    d proper meals   e didn't object   f argument

Looking at story settings
  6 Was the new house neat and tidy or a mess? How do you know?
  7 Was everyone friendly or cross? How do you know?
  8 Why do you think 'the dog had run away twice'?
  9 Why do you think there was newspaper 'all over the place'?
  10 How would you have felt if you had been there that day? Give your reasons.

Extra

Imagine you are Marion or Simon. You are in bed when the ghost comes out of the drawer. Write about:
- what you say
- what you do
- how you feel.

Unit 2

Finding the facts
▸ Navigating information texts
▸ Finding information

Looking for information

There are two parts of a **non-fiction** book that are very important. The first part, called the Contents, comes at the beginning of the book.

This is the Contents page of a book called *All About Animals*.

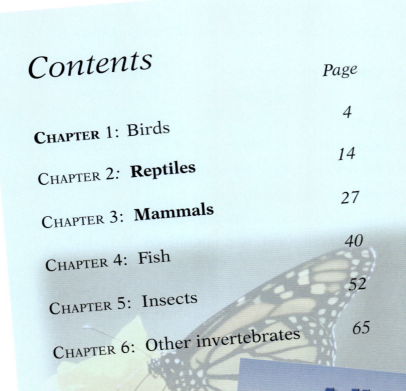

Contents

	Page
CHAPTER 1: Birds	4
CHAPTER 2: **Reptiles**	14
CHAPTER 3: **Mammals**	27
CHAPTER 4: Fish	40
CHAPTER 5: Insects	52
CHAPTER 6: Other invertebrates	65

The second part, called the Index, comes at the back of the book.

This is the Index in a book called *All About Animals*.

Index

	Page
	11
albatross	30
armadillo	36
bear	28
camel	16
crocodile	27
dog	6
eagle	31
elephant	35
giraffe	29
jackal	34
kangaroo	55
ladybird	44
marlin	58
moth	10
osprey	7
penguin	19
snake	9
swallow	53
termite	31
tiger	67
woodlouse	

Teach

- What is the book called?
- Where will you find the Contents page?
- Where will you find the Index?
- Look at the Contents page. How is the information ordered?
- Look at the Index. How is the information ordered?
- What do the words in **bold** mean?
- On the Contents page the chapters are about different types of animals. Now look at the Index. In which chapter can you find information about these animals? albatross - camel - marlin - snake - woodlouse
- In which chapters would you put information about these animals? alligator - beetle - robin
- Why do you think the Contents page and the Index are useful parts of a book?

Unit 2

What's out in space?

	Page
Chapter 1:	2
Chapter 2:	11
Chapter 3:	23
Chapter 4:	35
Chapter 5:	42

Understanding the Contents page
- What is the book called?
- How many chapters does it have?
- What page does Chapter 3 begin on?
- What page does Chapter 4 end on?
- Which is the longest chapter?

Looking at words

Explain the meaning of these words as they are used in the extract:

space   planet   satellite

Understanding chapters

As you can see, the chapters have no titles. Look at the information you can find in each chapter.

→ Chapter 1 has information on the planet we live on.

→ Chapter 2 has information on our satellite.

→ Chapter 3 has information on Jupiter, Saturn and Uranus.

→ Chapter 4 has information on rockets and the Space Shuttle.

→ Chapter 5 has information on our Sun.

- Think of an interesting title for each chapter.
- Think of three other things that you might like to read about in this book. They will be Chapters 6, 7 and 8. Give these chapters interesting titles as well.

 Extra

- Choose a non-fiction book from your class or school library. How many chapters does the book have? What is the title of the first chapter? Which chapters sound the most interesting? Why?
- Read out each chapter name from your book and discuss which group to put it in: 'useful', 'interesting' and 'neither useful nor interesting'.

Sport For All!

Here is the Contents page and the Index for a book called *Sport for All!*

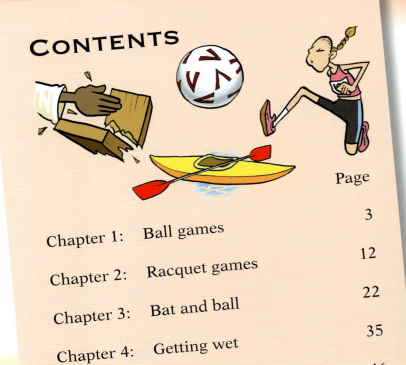

CONTENTS

		Page
Chapter 1:	Ball games	3
Chapter 2:	Racquet games	12
Chapter 3:	Bat and ball	22
Chapter 4:	Getting wet	35
Chapter 5:	Running shoes	46

INDEX

	Page
badminton	13
cricket	24
diving	37
football	10
hurdling	51
netball	4
rugby	11
running	48
swimming	44
table tennis	32
tennis	20

Write

Understanding the Contents page and the Index
1. What is the book called?
2. How many chapters does it have?
3. What can you read about in Chapter 3?
4. On what page can you read about:
   a netball   b cricket   c running?

Looking at words
5. Explain the meaning of these words:
   a racquet   b badminton   c hurdling

Using the Contents page and the Index
6. If you were interested in these sports, which chapter would you read?
   a swimming   b tennis   c football
7. Why do you think Chapter 4 is called 'Getting wet'?
8. What two sports can you read about in Chapter 5? What pages are they on?
9. Here are some other sports:
   volleyball   rounders   deep-sea diving
   a Which chapter would you put each sport in?
   b After which word in the Index would you put each sport?

Extra
Chapter 6 is going to be about the different clothes you wear to do different sports. Make a list of at least five kinds of sports clothes.
- Think of an interesting title for the chapter.
- After which words in the Index would you put the name of the clothes?

Unit 3

Odd-looking poems!
▸ Understanding the meaning of shape poems

The Shape I'm In

THE SHAPE I'M IN

Come and see the shape I'm in

Tall as a tale

Thin as a pin

w i d e as a smile

Bright as a tin

Dark as a cave

Curved as a wave

Wild as the rain

strong

I'm *this* and *that*

I'm here   I'm there

I'm eveRything

&

eveRywhere

James Carter

Teach

Cats Can

Cats can stretch
And cats can curl
Cats can pounce
And twirl twirl
Cats can sit
And cats can laze
And purr
A sleepy haze

Coral Rumble

- What is 'The Shape I'm In' about?
- Does this look like an ordinary poem?
- What is different about it?
- Pick out the rhyming words in the poem.
- Pick out the words that are written in a strange way. Can you say why they are written this way?
- The poet is writing about himself. Can you describe him?

....

- What is 'Cats Can' about?
- What types of words tell you what the cats do?
- Which of the two poems do you prefer? Why?

Rhythm Machine

This poem is about all the sounds a synthesizer can make.

Soft and
Humming
LOUD

And *strumming* –

Listen to this NEAT **refrain**

Add a **TRUMPET**

And a **DRUM** kit –

Why not change the **BEAT** again?

UP THE VOLUME

Eardrum priser

INSTANT POP GROUP

Synthe**siz**er

Trevor Harvey

Understanding the poem
- The poem is about all the sounds a 'synthesizer' can make. What is a synthesizer?
- What other musical instruments are in the poem?
- What does 'up the volume' mean?
- List the rhyming words in the poem.

Looking at words

Explain the meaning of these words as they are used in the poem:

strumming   refrain   beat
volume   instant

Exploring the poem
- Look at each word that is written in a strange way. Discuss why you think it is written in that way.
- Why do you think pop groups use synthesizers?
- Do you like this poem or not? Explain why.

 Extra

Practise reading the poem out loud. Try to make your voice match the way the words are written.

Unit 3

Stereo Headphones

I'm sitting on a train and I'm wearing my stereo headphones. And I'm putting on my favourite tape and pressing "PLAY".

SSSSSSS
BOOM
THUMPITY
TWANG
BIPPITY
KERBOP
BOOOOM

SSSSSSS
BOOM
THUMP
KERRANG
BOOOOP
KERTWANG
BOOOOM

Why's everyone staring at me?

James Carter

Write

Understanding the poem
1 Where is the poet?
2 What is he wearing?
3 What is he listening to?
4 Is he on his own?

Looking at words
5 Explain the meaning of these words as they are used in the poem:
  a stereo   b headphones   c favourite

Exploring the poem
6 Does the poem look like an ordinary poem? What does the shape of the poem look like?
7 Two lists of words begin with 'SSSSSSSSS'. What do these lists of words make you think of?
8 Pick out the sounds in the list that could be made by a drum.
9 Why do you think everyone is staring at him?

Extra
Choose a musical instrument and draw it.
• Think of words that describe the sounds it makes.
• You can make up your own words.
• Write the words inside the drawing.

Unit 4

Let's find out!
▸ Understanding and retrieving information
▸ Non-fiction text organisation

Great walls of the world

What do you know about famous walls? Let's look at three famous walls from around the world.

The Great Wall of China
The Great Wall of China is 2,400 km long. It is the biggest thing ever built by man. The Chinese began to build it in 214 BC to keep other people out of their country. It is about 9 m high and has lots of watchtowers all along it.

The Wailing Wall
The Wailing Wall is the only part of the Temple of Jerusalem that is still standing. The Temple was built in 950 BC and destroyed by the Romans in AD 70. Jewish people come to the Wailing Wall to pray.

Hadrian's Wall
Hadrian's Wall runs across the north of England from the River Tyne to the River Solway. It was built by the Romans in AD 122 to keep out the Scottish tribes. It was 120 km long but much of it has been destroyed. Along the wall were 16 large forts.

- How high is the Great Wall of China?
- What do you think a watchtower was used for?
- Where is the Wailing Wall?
- What is the name of the wall in the north of England?
- How many steps does the Leaning Tower of Pisa have?
- Which tower was a prison?
- Which tower is made of metal?
- Which wall is longer – the Great Wall of China or Hadrian's Wall?
- Which of the three towers was built last?
- What else would you like to know about these walls and towers?
- Look at the information on walls. Why do you think the writer has used headings and photographs?
- Look at the information on towers. How has the writer set it out?

Name	Information
Leaning Tower of Pisa, Pisa, Italy 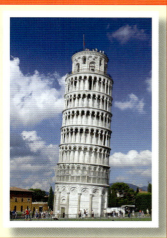	It was begun in 1174. It is about 55m high and has 294 steps. At the top there are seven bells. It leans over by about 5m.
Tower of London, London, England 	The tower is on the north bank of the River Thames. It was begun in the 11th century. It has been a royal palace and a prison. Now it is open to the public and you can see the Crown Jewels there.
Eiffel Tower, Paris, France 	This is a metal tower built in 1889. It is 300m high and was the tallest building in the world until 1930. Lots of people visit Paris to see the Eiffel Tower.

The world's great canals

Canals are man-made. They usually link two natural areas of water, like two seas. People have made canals for thousands of years so they could get from one place to another by water.

The Suez Canal

This canal was built in Egypt. It was opened in 1869. It connects the Red Sea with the Mediterranean Sea. The canal is 165 km long. Ships can now get from the Mediterranean Sea to the Red Sea and back again without having to go all the way around Africa.

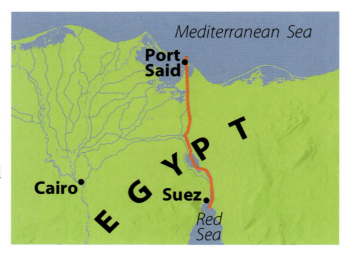

 Understanding the passage
- Where is the Suez Canal?
- Where is the Panama Canal?
- Which two seas does the Suez Canal link?
- Which two oceans does the Panama Canal link?
- What sort of transport uses canals?

Looking at words

Explain the meaning of these words as they are used in the passage:

link   natural   connects

The Panama Canal

The Panama Canal was built in Central America. It connects the Atlantic Ocean with the Pacific Ocean. It was opened in 1914.

The canal is 82 km long. Ships can now get from the Atlantic Ocean to the Pacific Ocean and back again without having to go all the way around South America.

Understanding information writing
- What do you think 'man-made' means?
- Which of the two canals is longer?
- Which of the two canals is older?
- Why do you think the writer has used maps?
- Do canals make a journey shorter or longer? Why?

 Extra

If you were the captain of a large ship, what else would you like to know about the Suez Canal and the Panama Canal?

Write a list of questions.

Where could you look for the answers?

Let's find out about bridges

There are many famous bridges in the world. This chart tells you facts about some of them.

Name	Where built	When	Interesting facts
Golden Gate Bridge	San Francisco, United States of America	1937	It is 1280 m long. It is a suspension bridge for road traffic across San Francisco Bay. It was the longest bridge in the world until 1964.
Humber Bridge	River Humber, England	1981	The bridge links Yorkshire and Lincolnshire. It was the longest suspension bridge in the world until 1998. It is 1410 m long.
Sydney Harbour Bridge	Sydney, Australia	1932	The bridge links the two shores of Sydney. It is 1160 m long.

Write

Understanding the chart
1. How many bridges does the chart give you information about?
2. Where is the Golden Gate Bridge?
3. Which two counties does the Humber Bridge link?
4. When was it built?
5. Which country is the Sydney Harbour Bridge in?

Looking at words
6. Explain the meaning of these words and phrases as they are used in the chart:
   a suspension bridge b harbour c shores

What can you work out?
7. Put the bridges in:
   a order of date when built, starting with the oldest.
   b order of length, starting with the longest.
8. Which bridge crosses a river?
9. What do you think happened in 1964 and 1998?
10. Sydney Harbour Bridge links the 'two shores of Sydney'. What is the bridge built over?
    a a river b a bay c a sea

Extra

The longest suspension bridge in the world is now The Akashi-Kaikyo Bridge in Japan. What can you find out about it?

Unit 5

Perseus's quest
▶ Investigating features of myths and legends

Perseus is given the quest

*Long, long ago, there lived a young man called Perseus. He lived with his mother Danae. A **cruel** and wicked King wanted to marry Danae but she refused. The King thought that Danae would change her mind if she were all alone in the world. He thought of a test for Perseus – a **quest** that was so dangerous that Perseus was sure to be killed!*

The King held a great feast. He invited a lot of rich people and he also invited Perseus. The rich people brought him gifts. Perseus was poor and had nothing to give the King. He was so **ashamed** that he promised to find the thing the King most wanted and bring it to him.

The King smiled **slyly** to himself. This is just what he wanted. He turned to Perseus and said, 'Young man, the thing I most want would take you on a long and dangerous journey. Other people have tried but no one has succeeded.'

'I will succeed,' cried Perseus. 'It does not matter that the journey is long and dangerous. I will go and bring you back what you most want. Tell me, what is it that I must bring you?'

'I want you to bring me the head of the Gorgon, Medusa!' said the King.

Everyone in the room fell silent.

Everyone in the room knew about Medusa. She was one of three horrible sisters. Her head was covered in hissing snakes instead of hair. Anyone who looked into her eyes would be turned to stone!

Perseus knelt before the King. 'I will bring you the Gorgon's head,' he promised.

Everyone in the room began to laugh. No one thought that Perseus could succeed. He would fail in his quest and be killed!

Perseus left the feast and went to sit by the sea to think about what he had promised. He knew that he had been foolish. How could he bring back the Gorgon's head?

Just then, two gods came to him. Hermes was tall and slim with winged sandals on his feet. Athene wore a shining helmet and smiled kindly at Perseus. 'We have come to help you,' she said. 'I will give you the sharpest sword in the world.'

'And I will give you my gleaming shield,' said Hermes. 'Look at Medusa's **reflection** in the shield and you will not be turned to stone. Others will help you in your quest. You must visit the Grey Sisters and the Nymphs who live at the back of the North Wind.'

'Begin your quest, Perseus,' said Athene. 'Be bold and brave and you will succeed.'

Perseus, retold by Wendy Wren

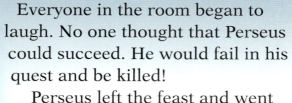

- What was Perseus's mother called?
- Why did the King give Perseus such a dangerous test?
- What was the test?
- What did Medusa look like?
- Who helped Perseus and what did they give him?
- What do the words in **bold** mean in the context of the story?
- Why did Perseus say he would bring the King what he most wanted?
- What sort of person do you think Perseus was?
- What sort of person do you think the King is?
- Do you think Perseus will succeed? What do you think will happen if he brings back the head of Medusa?
- If you were Perseus, would you have gone on the quest? Why? Why not?

The quest begins

With the gleaming shield and the sharpest sword in the world, Perseus set off on his quest.

Hermes had told him to go to a lonely cave where he would find the Grey Sisters. They knew where the Nymphs lived. The Grey Sisters were very strange. They had one eye and one tooth between them. Perseus found them sitting at the mouth of their cave, talking and passing the eye from one to another. Quickly, Perseus stretched out his hand and took the eye.

'Sisters,' he said, 'I have your eye. You must tell me what I want to know or I will go away and leave you in darkness.'

'We will tell you, we will tell you,' they cried, 'anything you want to know but give us back our eye!'

'I need to know where I can find the Nymphs.'

Understanding the passage
- Where did Perseus go first?
- What was strange about the Grey Sisters?
- How did Perseus make the Sisters tell him where the Nymphs lived?
- Why did the Nymphs give Perseus shoes, a magic bag and a magic cap?
- What was the place like where Medusa lived?

Looking at words

Explain the meaning of these words as they are used in the story:

gleaming   darkness   immediately   invisible

The Grey Sisters told him immediately how to get to the magic land at the back of the North Wind. Perseus gave them back their eye and went on his way.

Soon he reached the lovely garden where the Nymphs lived. He told them about his quest and asked for their help. They lent him shoes that would carry him quickly away from Medusa's sisters and a magic bag that he could use to carry the Gorgon's head.

'You will also need this,' said one of the Nymphs. 'This is a magic cap. If you wear this you will be invisible.'

Perseus now had everything he needed. He said goodbye to the Nymphs and thanked them for their kindness. He left the beautiful garden and began his journey to the wild, stony land where Medusa and her sisters lived.

Perseus, retold by Wendy Wren

Exploring the quest

- Outline the sequence of places Perseus has visited on his quest so far. What happened in each place?
- Why didn't Perseus go to where the Nymphs lived straight away?
- Do you think Perseus should have taken the eye? Why? Why not?
- How would you describe how the Nymphs treated Perseus?
- Why do you think the magic cap would be useful?
- How do you think Perseus was feeling when he left the beautiful garden?

 Extra

Discuss why you think Perseus will or will not be successful in his quest.

Perseus meets Medusa

After his long journey, Perseus finally arrives at the Gorgon's lair.

As Perseus came near to where the Gorgons lived, he saw statues of men and animals that had been turned to stone. Then he saw a frightening sight! The three Gorgons were lying asleep in the sun. He knew which one was Medusa as her head was covered in hissing snakes.

Quickly and quietly, Perseus put on the cap that made him invisible. He held up the gleaming shield and looked at Medusa's reflection in it. He drew the sharpest sword in the world and with one mighty blow, cut off her head. He picked it up and put it into the magic bag.

The snakes hissed loudly and woke up Medusa's sisters. They saw what had happened and jumped up. As they tried to grab Perseus, he jumped into the air and the magic shoes took him swiftly away. They followed him, screaming with rage, but the shoes were too quick for them. Perseus escaped and returned to his homeland.

When he got there, he found that all was not well. His mother had been made a slave by the wicked King. Perseus knew what he had to do. The King would think Perseus was dead. He would not be expecting the young man to turn up at the palace.

Perseus visited the King at the palace. All those who had laughed at him were there. One of them said, 'Well, well, here is Perseus. Have you brought the Gorgon's head with you?' And they all laughed again.

Perseus walked up to the King who said, 'So you have come back. Have you brought me my present?'

'Indeed I have,' said Perseus. He pulled Medusa's head out of the bag and held it up for all to see. Perseus made sure he did not look at it but those who did turned to stone. The King was one of them, and on his stone face was a look of fear and disbelief!

Perseus, retold by Wendy Wren

Understanding the passage
1. How did Perseus know which Gorgon was Medusa?
2. What did he do first?
3. Why did Medusa's sisters wake up?
4. What had happened to Perseus's mother?
5. What had happened to the King?

Looking at words
6. Explain the meaning of these words as they are used in the story:
   a mighty   b swiftly   c rage
   d escaped   e slave   f disbelief

Exploring the story
7. Why do you think Perseus had to move 'quickly and quietly'?
8. What phrase in the story tells you that Medusa's sisters were angry?
9. Why would the King think Perseus was dead?
10. How do you think Perseus felt when everyone laughed at him this time?

Extra
- Do you think Perseus should have turned the King to stone? Why? Why not?
- Perseus's quest began and ended in the King's palace. Draw a map of his journey. Label it with where he went and who he met.

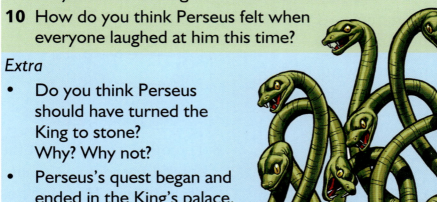

Unit 6

How can we do that?
▸ Follow instructions
▸ Understanding text organisation

How to play charades

This is a mime game for two teams. Each team has three players.

What you need:

- a piece of A4 paper
- scissors
- pens or pencils
- a watch with **a second hand**

Instructions

1 Cut the paper into three strips.

2 Think of the names of TV programmes and books.

3 Choose three and write one on each strip of paper.

4 Fold each strip so that the writing cannot be seen.

5 **Swap** your strips of paper with the other team.

6 One of your team picks a strip of paper.

7 Read what is on the paper and **mime** it to your team.

8 The other members of the team should try to guess what you are miming. They can't ask questions! If they guess in two minutes, your team gets a point.

9 The other team has their turn.

10 The winner is the team with the most points.

Teach

Some handy hints to help you:

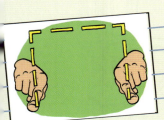
If you are miming a TV programme, make the shape of a TV in the air.

If you are miming a book title, spread your hands to look like an open book.

Use your fingers to show how many words there are.

For words beginning with th *(the / that / this / these, etc.)* make a T shape with your hands.

For little words *(a / is)* use your thumb and first finger to show that it is a small word.

If there is someone's name in the title, pat yourself on the head.

- What are these instructions for?
- How many teams can play?
- Look at the 'What you need' section. What would you use these things for?
- What should you write on the strips of paper?
- How long have you got to guess the right answer?
- What do the words in **bold** mean?
- Look at the words at the beginning of most of the instructions, e.g. 'Cut', 'Think'. What sort of words are these?
- Why do you think the instructions are numbered? Would it matter if they were in a different order? Why?
- Most of the instructions are written in short sentences. Is this helpful? Why?
- Why do you think the writer has used drawings?

Unit 6

How to make chocolate fudge sauce

You will need:

125g of dark chocolate, finely chopped
400g can of sweetened condensed milk
100g of white marshmallows

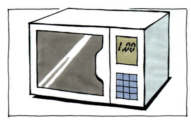

1 Put the chocolate and condensed milk in a medium bowl.

2 Place in the microwave and cook on medium for 1 minute. Stir.

3 Cut the marshmallows into small pieces.

 Understanding the instructions
- What are the instructions for?
- Why is the 'You will need' section useful?
- Make a list of the imperative verbs used in the instructions.
- What two things are mixed together first?
- What is cut into small pieces?

Looking at words

Explain the meaning of these words as they are used in the instructions:

finely   medium   mixture   smooth

Talk

4 Stir into chocolate mixture.

5 Place in the microwave again and cook on medium for 1 minute.

6 Beat until almost smooth.

7 Place in the microwave and cook on medium for 1 minute.

8 Serve hot or cold with ice cream.

How are the instructions set out?
- Why are the instructions numbered?
- Why do you think the writer has used short sentences?
- Why do you think the writer has used pictures?
- If you were going to eat it cold, what would you have to do when you took it out of the microwave?
- Do you think these instructions are easy to follow? Why? Why not?

 Extra

Choose a game that you play in the playground. Write the instructions for the game.

How to find your way!

When you want to get from one place to another but don't know the way, you can go on the web for directions.

Here are the directions from www.MAPTODO.com to get from the village of Greenly to the town of Bridgeton.

- Leave Greenly on Park Road.
- Turn right onto Frog Lane for 1 mile.
- At the crossroads go straight on for ½ mile.
- Turn left onto Grange Road.
- At the first set of traffic lights, turn right onto Bank Lane.
- Go along Bank Lane for 5 miles.
- Take the third exit at the roundabout signposted Bridgeton.
- Go straight on over the railway bridge for 2 miles.
- At the next roundabout, take the first exit.
- At the T-junction turn right.
- Arrive at Bridgeton.

Write

Understanding the directions
1. Where do the directions start from?
2. Where do the directions finish?
3. Do you turn left or right into Frog Lane?
4. How many miles do you travel on Bank Lane?
5. At the second roundabout, which exit do you take?

Looking at words
6. Explain the meaning of these words as they are used in the directions:
   - **a** the web
   - **b** crossroads
   - **c** traffic lights
   - **d** exit
   - **e** roundabout
   - **f** T-junction

Exploring directions
7. Make a list of the imperative verbs used in the directions.
8. Why has the writer used arrows?
9. What phrases has the writer used to tell you what direction to go in?
10. Do you think these directions are easy to follow? Why? Why not?

Extra

Write a set of directions for getting from your house to school or the shops. You could be walking or going by car.

Unit 7

Talk, talk, talk!
▶ Understanding speech in narrative and plays

Choosing a pet: the narrative

A small boy called Danny goes into a pet shop. He wants a friend!

   Danny walked into the pet shop. The bell on the back of the door rang as he closed it behind him and a tall, thin, grey-haired old man **peered** at him from behind the counter.
   'I'd like to look around, if it's all right,' said Danny in a small voice.
   The old man nodded and went back to **scribbling** in his notebook.
   There were rows and rows of cages all **stacked** up on top of each other against the wall, full of rabbits and guinea-pigs, rats and mice, kittens and puppies, parakeets and budgies and even a pair of chinchillas.
   Danny walked slowly from one cage of furry bodies to another.
   'Looking for something **in particular**?' asked the old man suddenly. Danny noticed he had a squint in one eye.
   'Um, well, er, I was thinking of a dog,' he replied **uncertainly**.
   'Any particular kind of dog? A short dog? A long dog? A fat dog? A skinny dog? One with spots, or stripes, or plain?'
   'Just any dog, a dog that could keep me company. I wanted to ask how much puppies cost.'
   'It depends,' said the man, widening his squinty eye for a moment. 'You see, all the dogs here cost two months' pocket money, whatever that might be.'
   'You mean, if I was given a lot of pocket money in two months a dog would cost a lot, and if I was given hardly anything, then that would be enough too?'
   'Got it in one,' the man replied. 'If you want a dog that's all yours, you have to pay for it. Two months' pocket money means you are serious and you'll look after the animal properly.'

Rent a Friend, Frieda Hughes

- Who are the characters in the story and in the play?
- Where is the setting?
- What is Danny looking for?
- How much do dogs cost?
- What do the words or phrases in **bold** mean in the context of the story?
- How do you know Danny is lonely?
- How do you know that the man wants to make sure Danny will look after the dog?
- How can you tell when a character is speaking:
  a in the story
  b in the play?
- The man says, 'Looking for something in particular?' How do you know he says it suddenly:
  a in the story
  b in the play?
- The story and the play look different on the page. What differences can you see?

Choosing a pet: the play

Scene: A pet shop.
A small boy called Danny goes into a pet shop.
An old man with grey hair and a squint is behind the counter.

Danny: I'd like to look around, if it's all right.

The man nods. Danny walks around looking at the animals in their cages.

Man: *(suddenly)* Looking for something in particular?

Danny: *(uncertainly)* Um, well, er, I was thinking of a dog.

Man: Any particular kind of dog? A short dog? A long dog? A fat dog? A skinny dog? One with spots, or stripes, or plain?

Danny: Just any dog, a dog that could keep me company. I wanted to ask how much puppies cost.

Man: It depends. You see, all the dogs here cost two months' pocket money, whatever that might be.

Danny: You mean, if I was given a lot of pocket money in two months a dog would cost a lot, and if I was given hardly anything, then that would be enough too?

Man: Got it in one. If you want a dog that's all yours, you have to pay for it. Two months' pocket money means you are serious and you'll look after the animal properly.

Rent a Friend, adapted by Wendy Wren

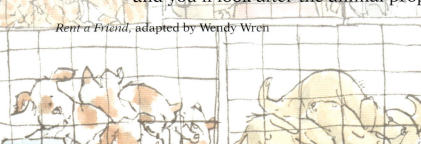

What is a Friend?

Scene: A path through a wood. Two friends, Adam and Seth, are walking along.

Adam: It will be dark soon. We should find somewhere to camp.

Seth: Good idea. *(Takes off his rucksack.)* Listen! Can you hear something?

There is a rustling in the trees.

Adam: *(pointing)* It's coming from over there!

Seth: Look! Look! It's a bear! Run!

Seth runs to the nearest tree and climbs to safety.

Adam: *(Struggling to get his rucksack off.)* Help me! My rucksack's stuck!

Understanding the play
- Who are the characters in the play?
- What is the setting?
- What are the boys carrying?
- Do you think Seth is a good friend or not? Why?
- Why do you think Adam pretends to be dead?

Looking at words

Explain the meaning of these words as they are used in the play:

    rucksack   rustling   safety   aid

Seth: Climb a tree, Adam! Be quick!

But it is too late. The bear is too close. Adam falls to the ground and pretends to be dead.

Bear: I cannot have the boy in the tree but I will have the boy on the ground! *(He sniffs at Adam then backs away.)* I will not touch a dead boy! *(He leaves quickly.)*

Seth: *(Climbing down from the tree)* Thank goodness you are safe, Adam. Did the bear say anything to you?

Adam: Yes. He said that the next time I go camping, I should go with a friend who will come to my aid when I am in danger!

What is a Friend? Retold by Wendy Wren

How is a play set out?
- What does the heading 'Scene' tell you?
- Pick out a short example of: **a** dialogue **b** stage direction.
- What lesson is the play teaching?
- If you were going to act the play on a stage, how would you make the stage look like a wood?

 Extra

In groups of four, act out the play. You will need three people for the characters and one person to read the title and set the scene.

The Village Dinosaur

Everyone in the village was excited. Something strange had been found in the quarry. Jed went along with everyone else to see what it was.

'It's a dinosaur! It's a dinosaur!' he yelled, throwing out his arms and jumping up and down.

The Parish Clerk, who was standing next to Jed, went pale. 'Don't be so ridiculous, Jed,' he chided. 'There haven't been any dinosaurs on this planet for millions and millions and millions of years.'

But Mr Holloway, Jed's headmaster, had managed to make his way through the crowd. 'Just a minute,' he said, examining the creature. 'Jed's right!' he said excitedly. 'It is a dinosaur! He must have been preserved all this time. He probably got wedged between two rocks and was buried by a sudden sandstorm. There must have been a crack in the layers of rock which have formed on top of him and air has filtered through. All very mysterious, I must say. I've heard of toads and birds, swifts and swallows, and the occasional nightjar hibernating, but this beats all! We might find an explanation one day.' He took a closer look. 'He's a young dinosaur by the size of him.'

'But he's huge, sir, really immense. Much, much bigger than an elephant, and just look at his long, long tail and neck,' Jed cried.

'Well, he could grow twice as large – to 80 feet or so long.'

'Phew!' said Jed. 'We'll call him 'Dino', shall we?' In his own mind Jed had already adopted the creature.

'That sounds a bit obvious, doesn't it?' laughed Mr Holloway. 'But it will do for the time being. Yes, let's call him 'Dino'.'

The Village Dinosaur, Phyllis Arkle

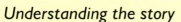

Understanding the story
1 What has been found in the quarry?
2 Who tries to explain how the creature got there?
3 How long could the creature grow?
4 What do they call it?

Looking at words
5 Explain the meaning of these words as they are used in the passage:
   a ridiculous   b chided   c preserved
   d filtered   e occasional   f hibernating
   g immense   h adopted

Exploring the story
6 Where is this part of the story set?
7 Who are the characters?
8 Who is excited about the creature? How can you tell?
9 Who is worried about what has happened? How can you tell?
10 How do you know that lots of people had come to the quarry?

Extra
Set out the story as a play. Look at what the characters do and how they speak to help you write your stage directions.
Look back at 'What is a Friend?' to remind you how a play looks on the page.

Unit 8

You have to read this!
▶ Exploring language in letters

Writing about books

27, Farmway
Kenning
KG4 X33

- What are the three different types of writing?
- Who is Mark writing to and what is he writing about?
- Did he like the book? How can you tell?
- Who would Mark like to be? Why?

Dear Ms Franks,

   I have just finished reading your book, 'The Whispering Wizard' and I am writing to tell you how much I **enjoyed** it.

   I have read all of your books and I was given 'The Whispering Wizard' for my birthday. I couldn't put it down until I had finished it!

   The Wizard was a really frightening character at first, but then I realised he only frightened people who were **evil** and horrible.

   I would love to be Sam and have all those amazing adventures with the Wizard.

   The way you describe Castle Chaos is brilliant. Is it like a castle you've seen in real life or did you just **make it up**?

   I do hope you will write some more 'Whispering Wizard' books. Are you going to? Are you writing one now? When will it be finished? I can't wait to read it.

   Yours sincerely,
   Mark Wood

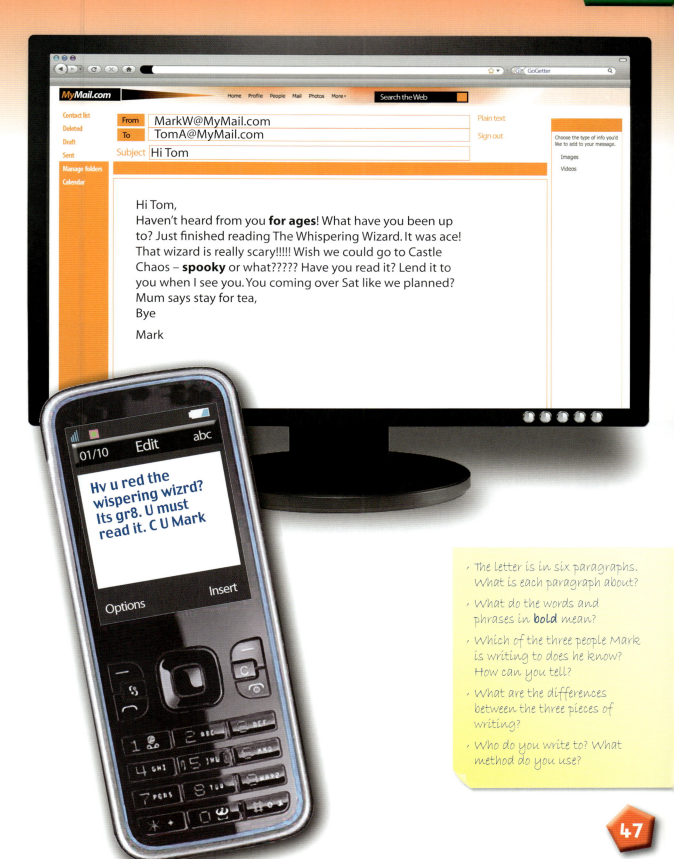

Have you heard?

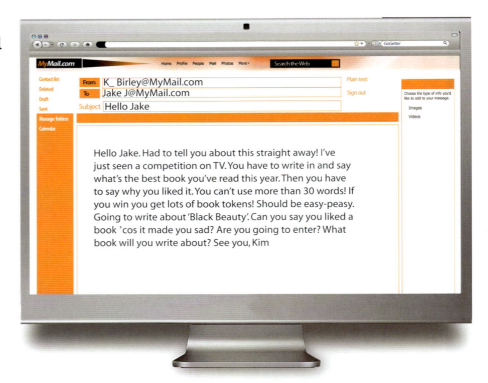

Hello Jake. Had to tell you about this straight away! I've just seen a competition on TV. You have to write in and say what's the best book you've read this year. Then you have to say why you liked it. You can't use more than 30 words! If you win you get lots of book tokens! Should be easy-peasy. Going to write about 'Black Beauty'. Can you say you liked a book 'cos it made you sad? Are you going to enter? What book will you write about? See you, Kim

Understanding the emails
- Who is Kim writing to? What is she writing about?
- What book will she write about?
- What book would Jake like to write about? What book will he actually write about?

Looking at words

Explain the meaning of these words as they are used in the emails:

| straight away | competition | easy-peasy | 'cos |
| loads | have a go | fiction | awesome |

How an email is written

Look at these sentences. Which words has the writer missed out?
a Had to tell you about this straight away! **c** Competition sounds great …
b Going to write about 'Black Beauty'. **d** Haven't a chance of winning.

- Which of the writers likes non-fiction books?
- In a letter, what word would you use instead of 'Hello' and 'Hi'?
- How would you end a letter to someone you knew? How would you end it to someone you didn't know?

 Extra

- Imagine you are entering the TV competition in the letter. You have to write to someone called Mr Parks, explaining which book you have read this year has been the best. Remember! You cannot write more than 30 words to say why you like it.
- Discuss what your favourite books are and why, then vote to find the class's favourite book.

What do you like to read?

21 Dee Avenue
Millfield
MD3 8YR
16th November 2008

Dear Editor,
I read your magazine, 'The World of Books' every month. I was very interested in an article in last month's magazine called 'What does your child read?' You asked people to send in suggestions of books young children would enjoy. I am a primary school teacher and I thought you would like to know what books the children in my class enjoy reading.

For children who like animal stories, the favourites were 'Cats in the Cupboard' by A. Evans and 'Elephant for Sale' by G. Brown. The children also liked the series of books about Gemma the Giraffe by L. Carter.

Most of the children like adventure and mystery stories, especially 'The Secret Island' by T. Fields and 'Mountain Adventure' by C. Clark.

The children also enjoy humorous books such as 'The Spotted Spider' by L. Kent and 'Where did I put it?' by S. Shaw.

I look forward to reading the list of books your other readers recommend. I'll suggest them to my class and see what they think!
Yours faithfully,
Mrs P. Richards

Write

Understanding the letter
1. **a** Who is writing the letter?
   b Who is she writing to?
2. What is her job?
3. What is she writing about?
4. What three types of books is she writing about?

Looking at words

5. Explain the meaning of these words as they are used in the letter:
   a editor   **b** article   **c** suggestions
   d humorous

How the letter is written

6. Whose address is on the letter?
7. The letter is in five paragraphs.
   a How do you know when a new paragraph begins?
   b What is each paragraph about?
8. Why do you think Mrs Richards gives the authors' names as well as the titles of the books?
9. Why does she use 'Yours faithfully' to end the letter?
10. If you were a teacher with 30 children in your class, how would you find out their favourite books?

Extra

Write a letter to the editor of *The World of Books*. Say what your three favourite books are and why you like them.

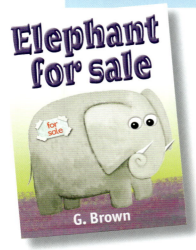
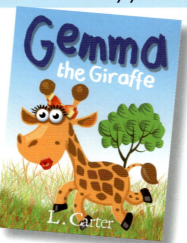
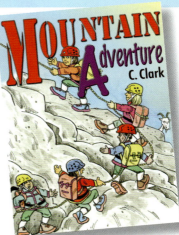

Unit 9

Can I change your mind?
▸ Understanding and retrieving information

Planet in danger!

- People were asked what they could do to save the planet.
- Here is what they said:

Have a shower, not a bath.

Use low-energy light bulbs.

Only boil as much water in the kettle as you need.

Save and use scrap paper for rough work.

Don't leave lights, televisions or computers on when you are not using them.

Recycle newspapers and magazines.

Don't leave the tap running when you are cleaning your teeth.

- We can group what they said under headings:

Energy	Water	Paper
Use low-energy light bulbs	Have a shower, not a bath	Recycle newspapers and magazines

- We can use what people have said to write a report on saving the planet.

Our **planet** is in danger. We use too much **energy** and waste too much water. We kill too many trees. What can we do about it?

Energy like gas and electricity is **expensive** and will not last forever. We can help to save energy by:
- using **low-energy light bulbs**
- boiling only as much water as we need in the kettle
- turning off lights, televisions, etc. when we are not using them.

Many people in the world do not have clean drinking water. We should not waste water. We can save water by:
- showering instead of having a bath
- not leaving the tap running when we are cleaning our teeth.

Trees are very helpful to us. We cut down too many trees to make paper. We can save paper by:
- **recycling** newspapers and magazines
- using **scrap paper** for **rough work**.

We all have to help to save our planet. What are *you* doing?

> **Teach**
>
> - What three things do people say they can save?
> - Give one example for each of how they can save them.
> - What do the words in **bold** mean?
> - Look at the report. It has five paragraphs. What is the writer talking about in each one?
> - Why is showering better than having a bath?
> - Why do you think we need to be more careful with energy, water and paper?
> - Can you think of other ways we can save the planet?

Unit 9

Save the rainforests

- has two-thirds of world's plants and animals
- absorbs huge amounts of CO_2 – the 'greenhouse' gas
- gives us many natural medicines
- tall, leafy trees
- not much **undergrowth** on floor = lack of sunlight
- **temperate** rainforests = away from **equator**, e.g. North America; lots of **tourists** visit
- animals/insects becoming extinct
- gives us timber / animals products
- world's rainforests are **shrinking**

Understanding the notes
- What are the notes about?
- Where can you find rainforests?
- Why are rainforests being cut down?
- Which rainforest has almost disappeared?
- Why isn't there much undergrowth on the floor of a rainforest?

Looking at words

Explain the meaning of these words as they are used in the notes:

undergrowth   temperate   equator   tourists   shrinking   oxygen

More rainforest notes
- almost 90 per cent of West African rainforest gone
- gives us 28 per cent of world's **oxygen**
- tropical rainforests = near the equator
- too many trees cut down = timber and room for people to live

How is a report organised?

These notes can be used to write a report on rainforests. Which notes would you use for each paragraph?

Paragraph 1: What do rainforests look like?
Paragraph 2: What are the two kinds of rainforests?
Paragraph 3: What does a rainforest give us?
Paragraph 4: What is happening to the rainforests? Why?

 Extra

Imagine you could talk to somebody who was cutting down the rainforest trees. You want them to stop. What will you say?

Make up some questions to ask and then have a role-play discussion.

Recycle with Michael!

Have you ever wondered what happens to our rubbish? Much of our rubbish ends up buried in the ground. Where rubbish is buried is called a landfill site. These landfill sites are filling up quickly. We cannot keep digging huge holes in the earth. What we must do is recycle our rubbish.

Local councils are helping people to recycle. Wrexham, in Wales, has launched a scheme called 'Recycle with Michael'. This scheme helps people to sort their rubbish rather than putting it all in one bin.

Each house is provided with different containers for different types of rubbish:

- Reusable green sack: this is for newspapers, magazines and junk mail.
- Plastic box: this is for plastic bottles, cans, tins, aerosols, glass bottles and jars.
- Green bin: this is for grass cuttings, hedge and bush cuttings, dead flowers and weeds.
- Grey bin: this is for non-recyclable rubbish.

The Council provides everyone with a calendar so they know when their bags, boxes and bins will be collected.

Wrexham County Borough Council

Understanding the report

1 Where does most of our rubbish go?
2 What is happening to these sites?
3 What should we be doing with our rubbish?
4 Who is helping people to recycle? What is the name of the scheme?

Looking at words

5 Explain the meaning of these words and phrases as they are used in the report:
   a landfill sites   b launched   c scheme
   d containers   e reusable   f junk mail

Understanding the report

6 How many paragraphs are in the report? What does each paragraph talk about?
7 How many containers does each house get?
8 Which types of house might not need a green bin?
9 Why is the calendar so important?

Extra

Think about all the things you throw away at home. Make a list. If you had the four containers which would you fill up first? Why?

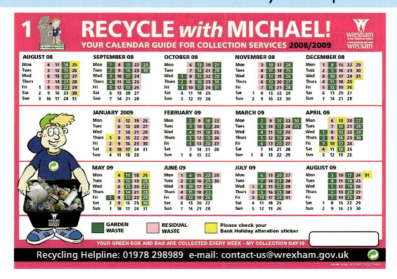

Unit 10

What's going to happen next?
▶ Understanding characters' feelings and empathy

Wanted: a real dragon

This story is about Jilly who wants a real, live dragon. She goes with her Dad to the Magic Shop to see if Mr Pink can help her!

- Who are the characters in the story?
- Where does this part of the story take place?
- What does Jilly want?
- What did Mr Pink get from the top shelf?
- What do the words in **bold** mean in the context of the story?
- What does Jilly mean when she says, 'I know it in my bones'?
- How do you know Jilly hasn't told her father the real reason for going to the Magic shop?
- How do you know Mr Pink doesn't look for things on the top shelf very often?
- What 'secrets' do you think Mr Pink will tell Jilly?
- If you got to this part of the story, would you read on? Why? Why not?
- Do you think Jilly will get her dragon? Why? Why not?

'I want a dragon,' Jilly told him. 'I know you can't buy them, but I'm sure there are such things. I know it in my bones.'

'If you believe in dragons,' said Mr Pink, 'then of course there are such things – for you.'

He did not sound at all surprised. He **behaved** as if someone asked him for a dragon every day of the week.

'Was there any particular kind of dragon you had in mind?' he went on.

'Oh, yes, yes!' Jilly told him eagerly. 'I'd like one just like the one on the poster in my bedroom. One with bright green **scales** and a curly tail. He's puffing out fire, but he looks really **tame**. He's smiling, I'm sure he is.'

'Well, then, you shall have that very one,' Mr Pink told her.

'Really?' cried Jilly. 'You mean – you mean you can bring him to life?'

Mr Pink did not reply. He fetched a pair of stepladders and placed them against the shelves. Then he climbed up, right to the very top.

'Let me see, let me see …' she heard him mutter.

Jilly saw him take a small box from the very back of that **mysterious** top shelf. Then, very carefully, he came down again.

'What a lot of cobwebs!' he said.

'What a lot of dust! I don't get asked for real magic everyday, you see.'

Jilly **glanced** quickly towards the window, to make sure her father was not peeping. Luckily he was still looking at the masks and tricks in the window.

Mr Pink took the large green handkerchief from his top pocket and carefully dusted the box. Jilly could see that it was very, very old. It was made of wood, and strange signs and letters were carved on it.

'And now,' he said to Jilly, 'it's time for secrets!'

Dragon Ride, Helen Cresswell

Meeting the dragon

Jilly takes the box home from the Magic Shop. That night, when her mother had kissed her good night and left the room, Jilly got out of bed.

She lifted the pillow and took out the tiny green package. She carried it over to the table. Then she went to take down her dragon poster. Her fingers were trembling. She carried the poster over to the table and stared down at it.

She had lain in bed and gazed at it so many times before that she knew every tiny detail. If she closed her eyes, she could still see it. What was it Mr Pink had said?

'First, you must name him.'

Jilly had thought about this all day. She touched the painted dragon lightly on the head. 'I name you Lancelot!' she told him. He did not stir. He was still fixed and painted on the paper. She was pleased with the

 Understanding the story
- What two things did Jilly put on the table?
- What was the first thing that Jilly had to do?
- What was in the tiny parcel?
- What did Jilly feel against her cheek?
- What was happening?

Looking at words

Explain the meaning of the words as they are used in the story:

trembling   detail   stir   invisible   unfurling   eager name. She thought it sounded good and dragon-like. You couldn't give a dragon an ordinary name like John or Mark or Keith.

Now came the most important moment of all. She opened the tiny parcel and stared at the pale green powder. Then, very carefully, she repeated to herself the words Mr Pink had told her to say. 'I take you, Lancelot, to be my dream,' she whispered. 'We will go invisible, like the wind!'

She waited, breath held, eyes still tight shut. Could it be, could it possibly be that, at this very moment, a real dragon was unfurling real wings from the flat prison of the poster? She thought she felt a stir of the air, a faint breath against her cheek. Half eager and half afraid she opened her eyes. 'Oh!' she gasped. There was the dragon she had longed for and dreamed of.

Dragon Ride, Helen Cresswell

Building the suspense
- How do you know that Jilly was excited?
- Make a list of the things she had to do before the dragon came to life.
- Why do you think Mr Pink told her to say, 'I take you … to be my dream'?
- Jilly is 'half afraid'. What do you think she is afraid of?
- Why do you think the writer doesn't just write, 'Jilly used the magic powder and the dragon came to life'?

 Extra

Imagine you could talk to Jilly about her dragon.
Make up questions to ask her about why she wanted a dragon and how she felt when the dragon came to life.

Flying with a dragon

Jilly's dream has come true! In her room is a real, live dragon and they are about to have an amazing adventure. The dragon tells Jilly to climb on his back.

And then they were off! She felt the strong upward beat of his wings as he soared through the window and into the open air.

She looked down and saw the garden below. She saw the roses, the apple trees and her father digging. She gave a gasp. What if he looked up and saw her?

'We are invisible, remember,' came Lancelot's voice. It was as if he had read her thoughts.

'So we are!' She felt suddenly free! Hurray! We can go where we like, and no one will see us. Puff some fire! Please puff some fire!'

Lancelot obeyed. It was just as she had dreamed it would be. Flames went forking out on all sides. They danced and curled like scarlet snakes.

'Hurray!' Jilly yelled again.

'What about some green smoke?' he called.

'Oh yes, please! Puff some green smoke. Puff lots of it!'

And so he did. Now the scarlet snakes were dancing in a green mist.

As the dragon rose higher and higher, Jilly could see tiny people walking below. They looked like toys. 'If they looked up, all they'd see is the moon coming up,' Jilly thought. They could not guess that right above their very heads was a dragon flying.

Dragon Ride, Helen Cresswell

Understanding the story
1. How did Jilly and the dragon get out of her bedroom?
2. Who was in the garden?
3. What did Jilly ask Lancelot to do?
4. What else did Lancelot do?
5. If people looked up, what would they see?

Looking at words
6. Explain the meaning of these words as they are used in the story:
   a soared   b gasp   c obeyed
   d forking

Exploring the adventure
7. Why couldn't anyone see Jilly and Lancelot?
8. How do you know Jilly was enjoying herself?
9. How does the writer describe:
   a Lancelot's fire   b the people walking below?
   Explain why these are good descriptions.
10. How do you know that Jilly had thought about a dragon ride before?

Extra
- Where do you think Jilly might ask the dragon to take her?
- Imagine you could go for a dragon ride. Write about where you would ask the dragon to take you and why.

How to use this book

This Pupil Book consists of ten units that help to teach comprehension skills for a range of different text types and genres, including fiction, non-fiction and poetry. It can be used on its own or as part of the whole Nelson Comprehension series, including Teacher's Resource Books and CD-ROMs. Each Nelson Comprehension unit is split into three sections.

Teach The 'Teach' section includes an illustrated text for a teacher and children to read together and discuss in class. To help guide the discussion, a series of panel prompt questions is supplied, which can be used to help model a full range of comprehension skills (such as literal understanding, inference and evaluation). Full answer guidance is supplied in the accompanying *Teacher's Resource Book*, with multi-modal whiteboard support (complete with voiceovers and a range of audio and visual features) on the CD-ROM.

Talk The aim of this section is to get the children in small groups to practise the skills they have just learnt. Each child could take on a role within the group, such as scribe, reader or advocate. They are presented with a range of questions to practise the skills they have been learning in the 'Teach' section.

Write The questions are followed up by a discussion, drama, role play or other group activity to further reinforce their learning. Further guidance is supplied in the *Teacher's Resource Book*, while interactive group activities to support some of the 'Talk' questions and activities are supplied on the CD-ROM.

The third section offers an opportunity to test what the children have learnt by providing a new text extract and a series of questions, which can be answered orally, as a class exercise, or as an individual written exercise. The questions are colour coded according to their type, with initial literal questions, followed by vocabulary clarification, inference and evaluation questions and then an extended follow-up activity. Full answer guidance is supplied in the accompanying *Teacher's Resource Book*, while a whiteboard questioning reviewing feature is supplied on the CD-ROM.